MW01518989

To JACK & JONATHAN,

When you two bite
into this book,
I hope all you taste
is love.

Ted Van E___

12/2012

WATER

EARTH

FIRE

AIR

Poems

EDWARD V. VAN SLAMBROUCK

EDITED BY CAROLYN WALKER

iUniverse, Inc.
Bloomington

WATER EARTH FIRE AIR
Poems

iUniverse books may be ordered through booksellers or by contacting:

iUniverse
1663 Liberty Drive
Bloomington, IN 47403
www.iuniverse.com
1-800-Authors (1-800-288-4677)

ISBN: 978-1-4759-4316-0 (sc)
ISBN: 978-1-4759-4317-7 (ebk)

Library of Congress Control Number: 2012914308

Printed in the United States of America

Contents

FIRE

AIR

This Book is dedicated in the memory of

Margo LaGattuta

Poetry knows no borders
its country is the soul . . .

Peter Meinke

Acknowledgments

Carolyn Walker has aided me with her wisdom, poetic know-how and editing talents in the task of writing and publishing *Water Earth Fire Air*. Her time, friendship and guidance are hereby recognized and appreciated with an unlimited "thank you."

My teacher and mentor, Margo La Gattuta, poet and dear friend, will always be remembered. She departed this earth last summer; however, she still helps me to write. The poem titled "Margo" was written the day after she died.

Within my family, I wish to give special thanks to my wife Diane who gives reason and rhyme to my life. Also, thanks to my brother Paul Van Slambrouck who has supported my poetic endeavors over the years. In addition, thanks to Joan Rivet, my sister-in-law, who read my raw poems and pointed out flaws.

Poets who have aided me one time or another, are Peter Meinke, James Ahearn, Shirley Steiman, Julie George, Polly Opsahl, Mono D'Angelo and M. L. Liebler.

Thanks to you, my friends.

Previously Published Poems

(Some of these poems have been slightly altered.)

"Words", "Love, Life and Laughter", "Trinity", "Life Will Flow", "The Silence of Church", "Where Would I Go"—*Opus in Chromatic Words**

"Uplifting", "Dissonance of Our Wounds", "Portrait of a Poet as an Old Man"—*Heart Music**

"White Pines"—*Lamb's Quarterly* (Winter 2012 issue)

"Delights"—*Peninsula Poets* (Spring 2012 issue)

"God's Love is Free", "Where would I Go?"—*poetrywordmusic.wordpress.com**

* = Books and web site by Edward V. Van Slambrouck

Foreword

Ed Van Slambrouck's book of poetry, *Water Earth Fire Air*, is one man's wise, sentimental, and some-times playful meditation, on God's love and the experience of His creation. Earnest as a child's devotional, heartfelt as a father's prayer, and occasionally touched with a bit of a tongue-in-cheek pun, Van Slambrouck's poetry collection, his fourth in an ambitious series fueled by a prolific writing schedule, explores God's bounty as he lived it in eight decades of life. Using the language of imagery and style (informed by his gift for music), the collection takes the reader by the spirit and coaxes him through such diverse experiences as what it means to adore a woman, raise children, conquer illness, appreciate a friend, play the saxophone, feel the wind and worship at the foot of the Cross.

From its first pages, Van Slambrouck, invoking his Catholic heritage, takes on the mystical and the profound, relating them to the everyday encounters we oftentimes take for granted.

"A splash of earthly water inserts us into a life of spiritual accord," he tells us in the opening poem, *Water*, only to lure us back in time, and into the personal, as he broaches the topic of *Earth*, "During World War II my dad had me working in a Victory Garden . . ."

In the third of the book's four segments—each one devoted to one of the elements—Van Slambrouck's gift for humor can be seen in the opening lines of *Fire*: "Dante pegged hell as a multi-level pit of fire/with humans and devils having at it/like the super bowl game with horns."

But if we feel ourselves laughing here, we will find ourselves reflecting on the fact that we are embraced by the holy as said the first line of *Air*. "Air surrounds us with the goodness of God." Van Slambrouck is a poet for Everyman, reminding us that we are spiritual beings, his every page illustrating the gifts of our Creator.—*Carolyn Walker, May 2012*

Introduction

During Lent in the last decade or so, I read the Bible about fifteen minutes per day, a short daily prayer in a church pamphlet and a chapter of a book written by a religious author. This Lent (2012) I have read two books: *Following Jesus* by John Shea and *Our One Great Act of Fidelity* by Fr. Ronald Rolheiser—both were soul warming. However, being an old engineer, I utilized the Internet—each day of Lent I read Fr. Richard Rohr's micro essays on life and its mystic essence that he publishes for his vast cyber audience. In the past, it took me three years of Lent to get through Pierre Teilhard De Chardin's book *Toward the Future*.

Concurrently, I wrote 30 poems that are in this book, *Water Earth Fire Air*. During 2011, I wrote about the same number of poems, thus doing the analysis I see that Lent was a provider for the muse. I've added a few poems from past years and some published in two of my other books, *Heart Music* and *Opus in Chromatic Words*. (Both are in soft cover and e-Book forms, as is this book.)

Surprise! A high percentage of the poems are of a spiritual nature, i.e., God's nature, of which we are a key part. However with some modicum of balance, I have included a few off-message poems to allow the reader a breath of other air. In addition, I've included a few memorial poems about close friends. Death becomes a frequent event when you are my age. On the other hand, we can experience the same Spirit while living as we will after death, given that goodness wins.

Edward V. Van Slambrouck
Easter, 2012

I

WATER

Water

like bread, is food for body and soul.
It looks and smells good in soup,
delights the tummy, replenishes our cells,
allows new openings in the dam of ideas,
lets me launch my boat to find fresh food.

Earth's crust is 72 percent water,
our bodies are 60 percent, our food
is 20 percent. Christ's words do not
water us down; they keep us alive
with spiritual wealth. H2O is a holy tool.

A splash of earthly water inserts us into
a life of spiritual accord: Christ-followers
pointing to a pathway of Love
placed in valleys and mounts of pain,
in pools and ponds of joy.

Mist preceding rain freshens our faces,
invigorates our souls, turns the stroll
into a fast walk making time speed,
although we want it to slow to allow
events to register in our hearts

indelibly, thereby brooking the gift of water,
love, family and friends for endless time,
while being with the Father of time,
seeing forever the face of God, feeling joy
as when one first sees the face of one's child.

Christian Music

Your image of God creates you.
Richard Rohr

God is my love teaching all to grant
those in choir or pew to sing His music
for His loved ones living the covenant.

Aesthetic and holy Gregorian chant
in monophonic voice touches hearts quick.
God is my love teaching all to grant

organ power by Bach to transplant
sad moods. God defeats sorrow in a time-tick
for His loved ones living the covenant.

Handel and Franck compositions incant
the Mass' grandeur aiding the brainsick.
God is my love teaching all to grant

gospel music sung with rhythm that shan't
demean praise for our Lord nor His rubric
for His loved ones living the covenant.

His infinite concert that sustains us can't
limit forgiveness. For us, He will handpick.
God is my love teaching all to grant
love for loved ones living the covenant.

Words

*In the beginning was the Word, and the Word
was with God, and the Word was God.*
                    John 1:1

When I become flesh in my mother's womb,
I become part of my God's love, which
guards me then and when, at three, a car
hits me square allowing me to moan not a word.

Sister Mary Gerard speaks of John's poetic
prologue in grade school and gives me a rush
of wonder. Brother Remigius speaks of
Hamlet's *words, words, words* in high school
that give me the thrill of poetry.

Through Him, my flesh becomes six words,
the names of my children. Through Him, Diane
is found—she becomes the word *love* for me.

The hematologist drills my hip to capture
marrow to discover if I'll have tomorrows.
Thinking leukemia, she withdraws my
miniscule white count. Father Jack's hands
hold my hip while praying words to Him,
who multiplies loaves and blood counts.

Through Him, I write words
Praising and thanking Him
for the gifts of poetry and life.

Trio of Love Reflections

1. *Accidents will happen,*
mom said long ago.
Are lives a random
set of loves?
My basket of loves
has no randomness.

2. My family and friends
float in love.
Our loves are like water
tumbling down
a pond's waterfall
to splash with smiles.

3. Why not love all skin colors?
Love Christians, Jews
and Muslims too,
even John Steinbeck's
tree-lover in
To a God Unknown.

Love, Life and Laughter

Sometimes I stub my heart with hard amour.
Then I'm surprised that I'm covered in love.
(Love comes while breathing foul climate no more.)
I'm loved by my Beloved with His truelove.
My life flows in wave after high wave.
Some give meaning, forming joy-filled new souls:
children of His image—kin who I crave.
My waves of life pulsate with highs and lows.

I do believe my God's humor in me
becomes truly valued, makes me happy,
softens my pain, allows delights to be.
Laughter's nectar is like a fine white wine.
Three line iamb pentameter poem's rhyme,
exist to urge light mirth in my timeline.

In Walks Jazz

Franciscans and Jesuits both think
God can be found in all things.
Me too—a palm tree, a clover leaf
built with three, a conch shell
with its mathematical spiral,
a six week old baby with wonder-eyes,
the love that binds pairs—you get the point.
It's God's presence in all.

He, through our cogent minds, creates
engineering spans, pills to stop pain,
hats with protecting rims or bills,
power from all kinds of atoms, eves
for homes, a mural of the Last Supper,
Respighi's *Adoration of the Magi,*
Hindemith's *Temptation of St. Anthony,*
a Strauss tone poem and musical
instruments for all to play.

Then, in walks jazz and God smiles.
Each chart coalesces in our brain,
becomes larger than the world's pain.
Seems like music seals God's love for us.

Word-music in poems leaps forward—
a line, couplets, Basho's three lines,
lyrics of Johnny Mercer, cantos,
poetic tomes, a plethora of forms
holding rhyme, rhythm and sound.

How can we not see God's hand in music?
Creative music channels sound-emotions,
sweet and sour, filling and empty—
a feast of all emotions that enables
His holy joy to be in us.

Have a dash of jazz for desert tonight.

God's There

The Catechism states that God is
everywhere. As a child
in grade school, the nuns embedded
that potent book into my soul.

If everywhere, then God is with me.
When I write poems, God is with me.
When I tell off-color jokes, God is with me.
When I go to jazz concerts, God is with me.

Certain tribes of American Indians
believed God lived in deep caves
in Mother Earth. When they buried
their dead in caves they left lit torches
for their spirits to travel in light,
deep below where their God resided.
Guess what, God was there.

Years ago, I visited Little Big Horn
where the Ogalala and Hunkpapa Sioux
killed Yellow Hair, took scalps from troopers.
My guess is God did not like that battle,
but you can bet that God was there.

The presence of God in humans
who tell tales of tragedy or cheer,
who do evil and good each day
has God shrugging his shoulders.
Then He throws more love our way.

Metaphor in Classical Music

The piece starts with the bang of percussion:
the xylophone rings each bar scaling high,
mining low to have a design of audio beauty
augmented with all sorts of aids—triangle,
gongs, cymbals both small and Chinese mammoths.
Finally, clappers, whistles, snares and blocks
all leading to an amazing crescendo
of thunderous timpani rolls—Trinity sounds.

The concerto of life can acclaim scores
sounding trillions of notes, each having
independent tones, each helping the notes
nearby, allowing harmony to flower
into spring's rhododendron bushes,
occasionally thorny Russian olive trees.

The concerto's honored instruments,
whether base violin, grace filled clarinet
or English horn coalesces into a community
of horns, strings and drums to create
a synergistic society of movements,
three, that give purpose to spirit of life.

Piccolo augments the wind with notes
of high order. Oboe doubles the reedy
flow of wind and water. Bassoon brags
about heterogeneous music in roaring
voice to set a baseline of fundamentalism.

Strings vary like birds of sky, with shrill tweets
and long deep-soul vibrations, while in between,
Yoyo Ma plays the melody that weaves orange
sunsets among clouds of human pain
ending in resolution as real as the cross.

God bless the brass, their angelic trumpeters,
the tuba tubes that wrap into our guts
with low notes, trombones that slide over lower
octaves of breath through cylindrical paths
in acts of faith for humankind. In the mid-class,
sets the saxophone moaning and wailing
between blue notes and grace notes.

Blossoms Beyond

Rhododendron leaves droop,
close during icy night, stay that way
until the sun bakes their bones
for reason in bud to blossom.

Hearts pump music from God,
the needed grace of guidance
to retain hope in waters of life.
Dare to go beyond.

All ages have doubt and loss.
Who gains when coveting tears
or breathing tainted air?
Dare to go beyond.

We roam within open hearts.
When we leave temporal life,
we fly into God's hands if
we've dared to go beyond.

Uplifting

Our church is in the round
like a Greek amphitheater,
only completely circular
with an altar in the center.

On this windy November Sunday,
my eyes are diverted outside by
leaf-dancing entertainment in a
corner of this church in the round.

Brisk winds coax dried leaves
to pile up in that catchall nook.
God's nature dismantles that
rabbit or rodent-leaved bed.

A tiny tornado peals layers of
multicolored leaves, spins
them skyward, mesmerizing my
mind. Up goes a ton of leaves.

Wide windows next to the roof
reveal those leaving leaves,
blown by a stiff west wind
to God knows where.

It's like our prayers going up
to God, to spread grace,
wind-wide, over Mother Earth.
That brings me back inside.

Who, Says the Owl

Presence is wisdom.
> Richard Rohr

Greece claims the owl as its national icon,
symbolizing wisdom. Traveling the roads
that Greek philosophers walked,
we see owl emblems on women's fingers,
on museum walls, on bed spreads
and in shops everywhere.
Much of the Bible's text is derived
from Greek translations by Christians
distributing God's infinite wisdom.

Humans need spiritual wisdom
to present in the present:
during chats with children
about their soccer games,
their craving for candy,
their need to pray and with adults,
when picking a movie, trimming
bushes on property lines, visiting
the sick, seeking spiritual wisdom.

When Medicare kicks in,
real wisdom tends to kick in,
ends embedded in the heart
in lieu of our mouth—
well not exactly, more in the mind
where an educated soul resides.

The Lord Speaks Through Flowers

They bloom with young colors these flowers
of God. Some blossoms are shaped like a bell,
others like snowballs, some stand out
like popsicles. These gifts have sounds
and bask in perfume, aided by the Lord's
humming birds and bees that spread life.

Friends applying love enhance our life
during trial or celebration, with flowers,
with prayer that pleads to the Lord
for less pain, more happiness, to ring bells,
to have family well, to have the sound
of laughter, to keep all evil out.

Grand-mom and the twins often go out
to the movies: animations of wild life
acting like confused humans, sounding
like chipmunks running through flowers,
living our history with humor. A bell
tolls the story's end—thank you, Lord.

Grand-dad and Mikey enjoy the Lord's
prayer at supper time; then they check out
the TV guide, hoping to ring Mikey's bell,
but it's all junk programming, no life
enriching stories or methods to grow flowers
nor any classical music with pleasing sounds.

Living or dying we crave the sound
of love, hope of being in the Lord's
hands. It matters not that we get flowers
at our wedding or funeral. It's pointed out
that God's love flows in death or life,
for both pull the rope of the church bell.

During youth, we dislike the school bell
calling us to book and desk with its sound
of discipline, yet it molds ethics of life
into our lives. Daily we wake to the Lord's
light which allows us to find out
our future, to see forever the flowers.

In life or death, we are the Lord's.
The temple bell stops, but the sound
keeps coming out of the flowers.

Note: The first line of the last stanza is from, Romans 14:8
The last two lines are a haiku authored by Basho,
the originator of that form.

God Soothes the Soul*

There is Spirit and therefore there is God.
There is Love and therefore there is God.
There is Music and therefore there is God.

We instruments are known by our rhymes.
Harp rhymes are sing, ring and string.
Cymbal rhymes are bell, well and swell
Flute rhymes are tooth, toot and youth.
Bassoon rhymes are pass, class and mass.
Dulcimer rhymes are grace, place and face.
Clarinet rhymes are clean, seen, and lean.
Saxophone rhymes are tone, moan and alone.
Trumpet rhymes are sound, bound and found.

God's trumpet is a blessed intelligence
for we instruments of His love.
God the Father plays Love melodies.
When we hear God's tunes malice ceases,
devils themselves are at peace.
His love is perceived in us
with remarkable stillness,
serenity of soul.

* This work is a modification of the recitative section of Benjamin Britten's cantata "Rejoice in the Lamb" taken from Jubilate Agno by Christopher Smart.

II

EARTH

Earth

During World War II, my dad had me
working in a Victory Garden at age 13.
All those seeds placed in Mother Earth
to incubate and become little green shoots,
then bushy carrot tops, bulbous red beets,
scallions for mom's soup, corn on cob—
sweet to the taste, tomatoes the size of Rudolph's
nose, rhubarb for pie, beans, peas and potatoes—
all nourished by earth, sun, rain and me.
Those vegetables of God's design enable
life, allow children to play in the sands
of earth between sea and land
where tractors plow, wheat grows,
reapers reap, which impedes weeping.

Life on our rich earth should aid the poor,
not cause weeping due to no home or money,
no food or medicine. Are we running improper
models on our computers—in our brains?
Would God agree with our models?
Half the labor force of earth works below its
surface, only a few work in tall buildings
reaping the wealth of all. Why, for God's sake?
Are we created to capitalize on others labor
resulting in unbalanced wealth distribution?
Earth, designed as a sphere, distributes land
in fat and narrow ways. Water flows over
the globe at an even level, giving all humans
access to its assets. I like the water model.

I Love a Mystery

It is the third eye that allows us to say yes
to the infinite mystery of Jesus
and the infinite mystery that we are
to ourselves. They are finally the same mystery. Richard Rohr

As a youngster, I clamped my ear
onto the AM radio to hear
"I Love a Mystery", a show
which gave me goose bumps,
then comfort when resolution came
at the end. Then it was back
to home work, night prayers and bed.

Strikes me today that those half-hour
stories were metaphors of our spiritual life.

The third eye is a cosmos gaze
that supports our spirit,
touches the infinite mystery.
The embodied infinite Love,
Jesus, aids us in solving
our mystery, resolving reason,
removing any floaters in our eye.

Trinity

"*God is a verb*"
  Buckminster Fuller

Mathematics is the Creator's tool,
I'm thinking, while driving through
paper mill owned stands of woods
in south Georgia. Was I taught that
in grade school by those chaste nuns?

Lots of math went into this car,
which smoothly traverses the asphalt
road. What about a Greek
triangle, the golden isosceles,
with a God-eye at the center?

Three sharp corners don't compute.
That geometry is not the trinity—
too much independence for three
in one. They each wear the same
suit, breathe the same spirit.

These small towns on Route 82
have a touch of England with their
single central roundabouts. That's it—
a circle, smooth, no start, no end,
ongoing, omnipresent, even cute.

Nope, cute ain't it. Fuller's idea
comes to mind, as I drive over a
speed bump entering a farm town
encircled by pecan orchards.
In a word, the Word is God.

If God is a verb of infinite action
who tags present time with *ing*
words, then what are humans?
I hope I'm not a conjunction or
a useless *the* or a fat adverb.

A preposition would be cool—
a *to*, an *in* or a *with*. Wouldn't you
like being someplace *to*
love a person? Wouldn't you
like being *in* love *with* someone?

White Pines

Trees can be like old friends . . .
we have been given all of these friends
as a gift from God . . .
He also speaks to us through them . . .
Fr. Jack Fabian

Iroquois' symbol of peace
is the great white pine tree.
Its roots spread throughout earth,
imagery of what God
is doing in and through us.

We children are more than reflections
of God's essence. We phone a friend
who is handicapped. We bake bread
and share loaves with the hungry.
We bandage a child's scraped knee.
We pray. We love. We cry. We smile.
We stir our souls to be immersed in God.

Nature is God's DNA, as is Jesus,
who walked in his Father's nature.
Let's walk in the peace of the pines.

Margo

And now I am waiting for my eyes,
waiting to clear things up, to see
what distant objects float by,
what bluer blue. What sky.
                    Margo LaGattuta

She has passed through that blue sky
to live in the light of the Word,
to breathe life anew in the warmth
of our prayers and our thoughts.

Life's like stanzas of a poem,
some good, some bad, some in between,
but all are raindrops from God's domain,
including his gifts of love and harmony.

Let his love take her into a cloudless future,
flow around her now, billow in her soul
for evermore, giving her bodily rest
while she writes poems about infinity.

She leaves unfinished lyrics in our hearts,
with memories of her grace and words.
Sky doesn't defuse her love
for we hold hers in ours.

Where Would I Go?

I mean your absence
would be a black hole
in my mind, too deep.
The space in this life
that God gave me
would be empty

of your breath,
leaving me only
memories
of love-linkages,
forcing my emotions
into an unnatural abyss.

How could I prevail
in that environ?
God would pull
at my bootstraps,
keep me standing.

Life Will Flow *

And life will flow like rich water.
Human consciousness on God's wind
ends on the bridge to everywhere,
while our bones lie bare and decay.
Though tears fall like comets,
though grave dirt grows grass day by day,
they shall rise again to realize
love's not lost and lovers remain
and life will flow like rich water.

And life will flow like rich water
on sea or land fed by the wind,
while the past remembers the dead.
Earth's green lifts spirit, chokes our pain,
gives reason not to break or bend.
Faith seeds new growth, disallows
Satyr's evil thrust toward our hearts,
aids the soul in its plastic shell,
and life will flow like rich water.

And life will flow like rich water.
No longer will crows cry in our ears
nor surf mist lie on face or shore
where petals flutter in the wind.
Lift eyes toward the sun, the Son.
Though they had angst and error before,
tender love pulsates through daisies,
breaks the mold to shine anew
and life will flow like rich water.

* This poem is "inverted" and parallel to Dylan Thomas'
poem *And Death Shall Have No Dominion.*

Delights

I long for the imperishable quiet at the heart of form . . .
Theodore Roethke
From "The Longing"

As you or I hug a fellow human,
we likely experience a form of God's love
exchanged to heal sadness, physical
or mental pain due to squeezing life too hard

or perhaps a happy meeting to add delight
from the Light. The quiet relief of love
from indirect sources allows you and me
to sense some wholeness from the Source

that never perishes, is always available,
ready to distribute more love while walking
barefoot on fresh cut grass, hearing the hum
of bee and bird, seeing the smile of a toddler

with a dripping ice cream cone,
smelling fresh sheets, feeling the kindness
of your mate, thinking about and having
those delights of life that link us with God.

The Mass Elements

. . . the bread and the wine. Both are paradoxical . . .
Fr. Ronald Rolheiser

The Mass is constructed to give us the living Christ,
couched in the music of the Eucharist. The Mass
is a human and divine story for us to live in:

The Kyrie:
Yes Lord, we need your mercy and your love too.
Jesus Christ, do envelope us within your mercy.
Gracious Lord, have mercy on us weak humans.

The Gloria:
Glory to God, who is most high in the cosmos and peace
on earth where humankind have good will. We do praise
You, bless You, adore You, glorify You, give You thanks.

The Credo:
I believe The One God, The One Christ son
and the Holy Spirit that flows between Them and to us
and existence of everlasting life with You Three in One.

The Sanctus:
"Holy, holy, holy, Lord God of Hosts:
Heaven and earth are full of your glory.
Hosanna in the highest!"

The Benedictus:
Gregorian chant augments the consecration
of bread and wine along with Bach and Mendelssohn.
"Hosanna in the highest!"

Agnus Dei:
Lamb of God, take away our sins; give us mercy.
Lamb of God, take away our sins; give us mercy.
"Lamb of God, grant us peace."

The Three are given to us to hold in our hearts
to touch in our mouths, stay in our minds and souls.
The Mass pours the Goodness of God into us.

That's the Spirit

The nature of God is to give Spirit into creation . . .
John Shea

Blessed are the poor in spirit, for theirs is the kingdom of heaven,
said Jesus on the mountain that glorious day. I've read where a possible
meaning could be: get up, go ahead, do something, move, you who are
poor in spirit to obtain the kingdom of heaven. My dictionary correlates
spirit to breath—perhaps hard breathing might be more accurate. How do
we give our spirit a charge?

He sits at the end of the picnic table in dirty, double-layered
coats since it is winter. He's talking with himself when a food bank
worker asks him if he want another hotdog. He nods yes, ends his self-
discussion and chews into his fourth dog. Some relish drops from his
mouth. He's alone in a sea of poverty with thirty-some indigents in this
soup domain where church workers calm their eclectic fears and needs.

Salvador, ten years old, wants an adult friend to buddy-up with.
Mark thinks that the church buddy program would give him a goal of
goodness. At their second meeting Sal gets four gifts from Mark—a 1944
aluminum penny, a shark's tooth, a stone with false gold glitter and an
Indian arrowhead. Sal smiles and his eyes drive joy into Mark's spirit,
which gives him a reason for the reason of Spirit.

Sophie has nine children, probably all out of wedlock. The Social
Justice Group learns that Sophie's rented house in Pontiac is flaking its
lead paint onto the dusty lawn where two of her youngest kids are playing.
They are munching on patches of grass peppered with flakes. Out come
ladders and brushes and the spirit of help to paint over the wrongs of
humankind, their goals of making gross amounts of money.

Using our spirituality is using God's love. It's using God's gifts to aid our brothers and sisters who are in plight. Preaching to people may be ego generated, yet for many, inculcation fosters help for God's children. (Hopefully, this gives me license to write this prosaic poem.) On a penny and nickel coin, there is a saying: *In God We Trust.* Whereas contracts involving money, voice no praises to God.

Life's Music

Music drifts in life's pulse and wind
while I wait for harmonious sweet tones.
We work and play and pray to the end.

Our instruments sometimes out of tune send
notes of heartfelt pain, hurting our bones.
Music drifts in life's pulse and wind.

Then again to omit sin we rush to mend
broken chords, to stop those throwing stones.
We work and play and pray to the end.

During movement two of our concerto, we begin
to solo in the band. That may lead to lonely zones.
Music drifts in life's pulse and wind.

Then some find in life that love must depend
on trust in others, the sound of God's overtones.
We work and play and pray to the end.

Our crescendos during life can transcend
our sins, bring the finale to the Tri-tones.
Music drifts in life's pulse and wind.
We work and play and pray to the end.

Mangers

I was surprised at the joy that I found . . .
Fr. Ken Mazur

The nun shows Father Ken the children
drawing pictures of the birth of Jesus.
He walks among the children looking
at their drawings. One boy has his stable
with cows, camels and people standing about.

Inside are Mary and Joseph and two
trough mangers. He ask the nun to ask the boy
why two mangers. She, confused too,
bends down and asks. The Indian boy
looks up into the nun's eyes saying

Jesus told me not to worry,
that if I was lonely at night,
I could sleep next to him.
One manger is for Him
and one is for me.

The Silence of Church

My priest uses his computer
connected to his piano to compose
religious ballads that hum in your head—
catch and hook your soul. I propose

to him *Grant me time with my sax*
in church to play in acoustic holiness.
His *Go for it* pleases my ear,
allows tunes that reduce my stress.

In the silence of church, my sax
speaks to God. I play my charts
while listening to the music
of His symphony, His art.

During my last tune
let me have wisdom,
rid the log from my eye,
let me have nothing to lament.

Love Stones

. . . the stones along the road
would burst into cheers.
                    Luke 19:40

Love stones are not from Gaul.
They are bedrock from God,
solid ground and distributed to all.

Love works in human spirit
when coupled with God's aid—
synergistic grace that counts.

Love takes me into a cloudless
future and flows around me,
captures my mind in life's dreams.

I like a warm blanket of love,
the one I find in our bed,
the one that covers all from above.

When we partake food of kindness
and love, it melts in our mouths.
It's absorbed. Love stones rock.

III

FIRE

Fire

Dante pegged hell as a multi-level pit of fire
with humans and devils having at it,
like the super bowl game with horns.
During mid-evil times, dragons spewed fire
from mouths with elephant-size alligator
chops ready to chomp off a leg.
Dante's idea was to place each category
of sin to a depth of pain in proportion
to the evil deeds done and the end results
the deed did or didn't do to people.

The Homo sapiens Neanderthalensis
had fire to warm food and family
to stay alive maybe 40 years. Fast forward
70,000 years to my backyard: my six
children are munching on marshmallows
around a bonfire, sitting on log and box,
telling ghost stories about non-existent events.
In early October, fire made from sycamore
tree sticks erases their daytime
tiffs, their homework stress.

Fire, a source of light and warmth,
a symbol of strength and energy,
enables society to fire Bessemer furnaces
resulting in steel products for both good
and bad use, for both pleasure and work.
Light comes from God's star sun,
from God's real Son, from His grace
called by human prayer and plea.
This trinity of stanzas stands in print
to proclaim the fire of God's Love.

Dissonance of Our Wounds

Our wounds bleed from illness, injury,
crime, tragedy and broken relationships.
Some wounds result from mistakes,
some bleed long with controlled grace

by inside and outside forces.
Wounds, over time, heal with scars,
the aftermath. Scars are part
of our lives even after death,

When scars transform,
no longer show a darker side.
They shine in transcendental form,
while we join our wounds with Christ.

Like musicians using dissonance
to produce song of elegant whole,
God uses dissonance of wounds
to create wonders in our soul.

Love's Trio

God is the Lover who gives Godself away perfectly.
Fr. Joe Dailey

Professor Sweetland teaches Greek history today,
asks his student what is philosophy. One guy raises
his hand to get a nod, answers that it is *love of wisdom.*
Sweetland's eyes get big and he blurts *in 30 years I have*
never gotten the literal definition. Sweetland seeks
in the soul of time, truths to be reseeded in young minds,
befriends his students with the Philia side of love.

Church seems a possible place to find a fantastic
woman in looks, demeanor and decorum. Raymond
inspects the prospects at the after-service get-together
crowd, hones in on a bench-sitting gem. Plato's Eros
is drifting about, driving Ray to chat with the ruby.
They date, have exposure to family and friends, which
leads into a lifetime of togetherness in all types of love.

No mixed metaphors here: Agape, the key love yearning,
the love feast that centers on others and opens us
to the supreme Lover who endlessly supplies his children
bundles of love to build cohesive relationships. This is
the love form Agape that links us to God the Father,
His son Jesus and the Spirit between them that thankfully
overflows into humans, while His children pray and play.

The Dance Band

Eight of us in Catholic Central's Dance Band
work religiously on Miller's chart
In the Mood. I have a solo on my tenor
and the gang says that it sounds good.
Though I'm the de facto leader, I don't
feel in the mood, since I like Kenton's charts.

Mike solos on his bone playing *The Song of India*.
Dorsey's OK, but I prefer Herman's tunes.
Besides, Norm drops his pegged tooth too much,
thereby reducing our sax section to two.
Brown's *Sentimental Journey* is mellow, sounds
smooth with Johnny, Norm and me blowing

in unison. Jack and Jerry on trumpet are brassy,
almost sassy during the bridge, while playing Duke's
Chelsea Bridge. Jack, with his piano background,
improvises on his solo, which helps our band
by adding a bit of professionalism. Jack is our star
football player too—that impresses the girls.

Our rhythm section has Bill on piano and Ollie,
on drums, who usually drowns Bill out.
Ollie's a Krupa wanna-be. He and I are birds
of a feather, both dig Bop, like Diz and the Bird.
These dance band guys cause me to think about
Goodman's *There'll Be Some Changes Made*

because the events in the above four stanzas took place in 1948. Today, I'm thinking *Swing Low Sweet Chariot* since Ollie, then Mike, then Norm are *Grooving High* and two more of us *Don't Get Around Much Anymore.* We remaining three are sort of *Blue and Sentimental,* however, we whistle *You'll Never Walk Alone* a lot.

Why Poetry?

Ophelia's father asks Hamlet what he reads. *Words,
words, words*, he replies, as known in the bard's book
of plays. The sonnets and plays are works of love,
force his pen to ink paper, to open his soul
to the ages. Do we read his emotions: fear,
envy, hope, anger or is it just plain joy?

Sure we feel emotions in writing—joy
is the dominant dynamic in art of words.
It was FDR who said: *We have nothing to fear
but fear its self.* True. When we write a poetry book,
we are like children playing, which delights the soul,
increases the wealth in mind, our bank of love

that craves more metaphors to enhance that love.
Similes too, are simple tools that inject joy,
but when one has keen rhymes it lights the soul.
Like: A man who wrote many poetic words
decided to frame them in a poetry book.
He knew in a Sestina there was a fear

that to not have fear in the ear, is a fear.
Fat fish in our vast ocean waters frolic and love
in the seas, lord it over those cats who in books
wander about to cull their food then eat with joy.
Full stomachs quell their needs for a while. Words
that they hear burn not their ears nor their souls.

Family memories are deep rooted in my soul;
they are in concrete, but the sledge hammer I fear.
I write poems of when I walk the woods with words
about my grandchildren picking tree flowers with love,
about my dog Misty who before cancer gave us joy,
about my affection for family. It's all in my books.

Spiritual side of writing is vital for writer and book,
for the heart bleeds then pumps pearls into the soul.
The New Testament writers ooze with unlimited joy
about the life of Jesus, giving us guidance, not fear,
giving us the way to find, use and enjoy His love.
The poetry in the bible is where reside His words.

It's not fear or pride that pushes the book
to creation. It's love that fills your soul,
joy of using that spirit of the words of God.

80th Birthday

1930 was a dismal year, so states the WSJ.
Not so, says my mom and dad on the day
I cried *Hello!* Well, I've greeted folks
galore during this eye blink. I'll stay

a while longer to continue climbing
the ancient sycamore, hoping to see
sunset of fulfillment from my branch
and the Person who created this tree.

From this vantage point, I'll continue
to shout *thank you* to family and friend
for being with me during my climb.
When I leave, I'll just be up the bend.

My commune pumps grace thru my soul.
You are loved, held close to my heart
where flows music of life, made possible
by the tuneful love that you all impart.

Contrition

Repenting is forever.
John Shea

I'm heavy of heart God,
for not following your guidance
of love. Please forgive me again.

When I offend you Lord,
who are pure goodness,
I fear loss of your love.

I dislike my negative ways,
for I wish your love forever.
I wish to reflect your love

in the way I live. With your help,
I confess and will make amends,
strive to do good wherever I roam.

I want repentance because I need
your free love to enable me
to distribute it to your children.

Prayer at Taize

I pray that God takes my pain.
God takes the pain.
I pray that God takes my angst.
God takes the angst.
I pray that God takes my love.
God takes my love
and returns it three fold.

The silence during Taize service
is broken by the honk of geese
flying south, giving God thanks.
Then an aircraft hums its way overhead.
Then children laugh in the hallway.

We sing songs conceived in France
with Spanish words, Latin words,
English words, all directed outward
from God's children, into the busy
cosmos of the infinity of the Trinity.

Another Lily Patch

My lily patch displays tall, redheaded
plants first. Two weeks later, yellow-
headed ones fan their arms sunward.
Finally, holy, white-headed ones
lift their pure faces toward God.

Those lilies have had their run,
overrun by weeds of time.
Our years add and add,
direct us to travel south,
away from God's frozen rain,
which blankets a thick white
on top of withered lily plants.

We play Up and Down the River
with condo friends in Florida,
while we wait for spring to peak
in Michigan. I wonder:
is the river the Euphrates
where God's garden once was,
holds fields of golden lilies?

Sister Mary Van Gilder, IHM

Shepherd me, O God, beyond my wants,
beyond my fears, from death into life.
                              Psalm 23

Mary, Mary, hardly ever contrary,
filled our lives with God's love
while mostly in pain, yet nary
a complaint or a why was in her love

for daily she breathed Yahweh's
grace of living our Lord's Word,
giving soft happiness each day
to those who hardly heard the word.

When I carried my dreadful cross,
Mary, sister and saint, said *Eucharist*
to direct me away from grief and loss
to gain spiritual love via the Eucharist.

Mary shepherds us into God's grace,
mending our spirit by using His words
of love which when directed at God's face
light our lives like heaven's songbirds.

Love

My heaven includes those I love.
Ronald Rolheiser

Love, the greatest essences of the trinity,
dominates the stage of life.
It forgives hurt, omissions,
and acts of evil error.
Love muffles faults, as do a mother's arms,
and allows sinners the warmth of home.

Love, spiritual DNA,
mysteriously heals souls
and links them to other souls
enabling symbiotic holiness,
manifested in family meals,
loyal friendships and shoes for the poor.

Love, given to anyone or accepted
with smiling heart, reserves
a place of honor in God's house.
The rush of God's love,
freely given or received,
defines the portal to heaven.

Love welds people to part of God,
bonds sinner and saint, cleanses
the sinner and promotes saintliness.
It's dressed in humanity
with the touch of a kiss or hug,
each a share of God's grace.

An Angel Named Diane

. . . but better than either, a devoted wife
Sirach 40:19

Bingo! Fate (think God) gives me
a superb gift, an angel without a wing—
her name is Diane. I feel like a king.

She, my Di, injects new life in me
and my family. My head, with joy, spins.
When she walks by, I hear violins.

I'm called the significant other, husband,
lover, and asked to empty the dishwasher.
You gave me this spirit of love for her.

Yep, I'm special Ed and Diane's the angel.
She reads the Bible an hour in the morning
while I sleep. She's praying, softly singing.

How wonderful Lord that you place Diane
here at my side among my six children,
and if I count right, eleven grandchildren.

Our rhythm and rhyme are blessed in life.
Dear God, herein I thank you for your gift
and having this poem a lot less makeshift.

Yet, please know my love is increasing
each year for her and You. I live in love.
We want to be with you someday, above.

Fishing in the Big Pond

In memory of Edward Kish

From the farm lands of Dundee,
to the plains of Hungary,
from the crunch of a hard tackle,
to the roar of horses on the sea,
from books of poems,
to sunsets on Erie,
from singing a Kentucky Babe to sleep,
to loving a wife true in life,
from chants in old St. Mary's church,
to comfort of kind kin,
from the death chill of Korea,
to the warmth of the Keys,
from the laughing truck limping about,
to tanks that tear at your soul,
from the thrill of the pike,
to the pull of the sailfish,
from a small boy with a bamboo pole,
to fishing in the big pond at His knee.

The steps of Ed's life forged friendships
here and there, wherever God resides.

When a friend stands at your side
he makes fast the present,
reaffirms the past,
helps us see the future.

Portrait of a Poet as an Old Man

Ah, we go into infinity for eternity.
I'll be delighted to be around
for that whole time if I don't get
trapped in a super black hole
bouncing from reality to anti-reality.

It's tough to bide my time when
I've got a decade of life left, if I'm lucky.
I say to hell with that biding stuff.
I'm going to pump, pry and push-out
as many poems as my computer will allow.

The woods behind our backyard
beckon me each spring to walk
among winter's broken trees, gleaned
by God's law as pegged in science.

When I'm culled by nature, I hope
the Designer will open the same door
that Martin asked to be opened in '68
when he said the day before he died:

I am a sinner like all God's children.
But I want to be a good man.
And I want to hear a voice saying
to me one day, 'I'll take you in and
bless you, because you tried.'

IV

AIR

I sit on dock's edge on Tampa Bay
viewing land's edge, water's fresh sapphire,
enclosed in air waiting for God's say
that has nothing to do about fire.

E. V. Van Slambrouck

Air

surrounds us with the goodness of God—
His 79% nitrogen, 20% oxygen & 1% mix.

Air designs ripples and waves on inlet waters
while pelicans sail on waves in drafty layers.

Air with its wall of winds, its blissful breezes,
flows from hill to hollow to mix with everyone.

Air cleans trees, distributes leaves, shifts
the desert's sandy sea, dances on fields of grain.

Air blows seeds for fish and fowl food,
elsewhere freezes a lost soul on tundra snow.

Air lifts up kites and kids; can be gusty as a slap
on the back, as refreshing as a cold beer.

Air blows birds high in the sky
to spy land-bound mice for meals.

Air has ozone holes in its 300 miles zone
through which rockets punch into space.

Air burns space junk, comet stones, meteorites,
while low red tail hawks dive for chipmunks.

Air cools as a dip in a pool, is still as an owl,
or still as an Egyptian in his tomb.

Air's invisibility aids our visibility—
we notice the warmness of our God.

Air breath of inhale and exhale proclaims Yahweh.
When we realize the NOW of God, we find new life.

Love Space

Open your eyes to all the love around you.
DOVE chocolate wrapper

Saturn's guidance computer holds complex
software, salient mathematics for silent space.
Programs guide humans to moon surface
like wind directing Columbus to the new world.

Writing programs (as writing poetry) charge
the mind like chocolate does the stomach.
Bootstrapping starts the computing process
as love sets offsprings' likes and dislikes.

To breathe on the moon is a small step
in breaths of life, love, and birth. My code
aided the moon effort; family codes aid
my children and grandchildren.

Mars will not mar our record, not inhibit
where we go or when we will arrive.
Nor will the sun's pull stop us in our longing
for answers, nor our love to have love.

Warping to planet Z333 or beyond leaves us
with the same question: Void or Love?
I answer love—God's love. We each will
choose an answer in due time and space.

Fresh Bread for the Mystical Body

Nothing is an island, not even a molecule or an atom.
Fr. Ronald Rolheiser

We live life in God's universe where robins
pull worms for protein, where leopards leap
upon four-hoofed beings who walk the river
bank where they drink the water that allows
plant life to multiply to be living food. Each
being strives for the means to support life.

We have God's DNA, perhaps a cell
of a finger tip or one in our aortic valve.
God's presence may be close as a droplet
of blood flowing through one's brain.
It's to be in His mystical body.

Adult human cell apoptosis is 60 billion per day.
In all living things, nourishment is required.
For us, fresh bread is best—the Eucharist.
(The name comes from the Greek word gratitude.)

We progress to the crossover, into knowing
that we are with God all ways, for sure when
we have forgiveness after a wrong we call sin.
God helps us to transcend physical, societal,
mental and spiritual problems in our life.

Dad's Table

Edward strikes me as a strong name
because Dad dubbed me with it, his name.

Dad had a game table made for playing cards
with a board that demanded chess or checkers

be the games of choice, the carpenter's choice.
The inlaid top squares had jumping knights

and sliding castles moved by his children.
Dad cut four inches off its legs to aid his brood,

which resulted in a slight wobble. After he died,
his table was given to me, his first-born son.

Edward was never used in my youth, Junior was.
When I started high school, I found Edward again.

The table was hardly used by my children
since I deemed it a loved gift from Dad,

not to be damaged by six combatants.
The table has a small drawer in the front,

with an ornamental handle, that today holds
pens, pencils and playing cards once used

by Mom and Dad. Now I'm over 80 and wish
to give the table to my last-born son, who

I named Edward. He has a technological lifestyle,
packaged with the welfare of his children.

I have felt Ed's love for 45 years. Ed will
treasure the table as I have—play cards,

checkers or chess with his two children, Sandy
and Edward #4. The caveat to get the table

from me is for Ed #3 to demand that he gives
Ed #4 the table and when Ed #4 has a son

that he, in turn, will will
the table to his Edward

I'll Go with Love

I'll go with love into that bright Light.
During late years, we may breathe rage
due to jaded age and death's ill fight.

Even weak men at end-time know right
from wrong, praying from age to age.
I'll go with love into that bright Light.

Strong men cry not about how bright
was life nor how care-filled is each page
due to jaded age and death's ill fight.

Sad men miss life's hidden thrills, the flight
into love, the feel of the sun's gage.
I'll go with love into that bright Light.

Grim men at end see with oblique sight,
hardly ever hold true Love or assuage
due to jaded age and death's ill fight.

And you, loved ones standing in my sight,
will know I've entered onto that good stage.
I'll go with love into that bright Light
due to jaded age and death's ill fight.

Note: This is a parallel poem that follows
Dylan Thomas' *Do Not Go Gentle into That Good Night*

First Born Finds Fun

Observing my first born during her first
20 years, reminds me of my early years.
We each took care of our siblings
with strong parental assignments.

First-born Kathy has concluded
that she should be awarded
a set of fun adventures
to compensate for the 40-some years
of being her family's chief worker

by compiling two buckets of fun.
She emptied the first bucket
in a few years and is eager
for the action in the second.

Bucket #1 contained these zippy-doo activities:

1. Zip-lining in the Appalachian Mountains—
the video shows glee-filled smiles.

2. Zip-lining in a St. Lucia rain forest in rain—
No video of her dripping and dipping thru trees.

3. Sky diving in Michigan—great video of a face
fearing, arms flapping, cheering relief at the end.

4. Hang gliding in Michigan skies over wheat fields and lake
cottages—she got the hang of it in time to feel the freedom.

5. Motorcycling in Michigan with pleasure and economy—Kathy's helmet, boots and bugs on teeth bring to mind *The Wild One* movie.

6. Snorkeling in the Caribbean—on vacation with her sister, Beth, trying to catch color-filled fish and perhaps some colorful male friends.

7. Kayaking at the top of Michigan's thumb—from Port Austin's pier to the Lighthouse and back, five lake miles, gaining arm strength. She can slam my hand down during arm wrestling.

8. Muddy Buddy competition in Rochester Michigan—sister-in-law Shawn and Kathy run, bike and crawl through a field of mud. The photos make me shake with laughter. But now I pray that bucket #2 reduces danger.

Art from the Heart

She aids the deprived by working
for the State of Michigan, Department
of Human Services. In her spare time
(read vacations), she adds to her
supply of God's grace, for she travels
to underdeveloped countries to build
shelters for the really poor. Our daughter,

Beth has done God's work in Peru,
Kenya, and Guatemala (three times)
where five new houses or churches
exists via Beth and her church groups
kind labor and humane smiles.

While in Kenya she bought three
ebony figures of Kenyan art
to surprise us. This year she buys us
an oil painting of the main street
of a poor jungle village in central
Guatemala. This art from the heart

has a background mountain,
which looks like Mt. Sinai.
The viewer stands in the middle
of a road which narrows
into an imaginary point. Each side
of the stone road has shops
and apartments, multi-colored walls
dotted with pots of flowers dangling

from windows. A distant church steeple
pokes the sky. A century old stone gate
stands crumbled, grass pushing
through. A newer gate stands over
the road as the dominate figure—

it shows pride and hope. The tile roofs
that roll the rain onto the rock road
appear on each side. Nothing is on the road,
not a person, not a cart or horse, not garbage,
not a dog or cat, not a can or beer bottle.
It is an accurate still life that needs help
from people like our charitable Beth.

Afternoon Practice

Big band with aged musicians
rejuvenate into new 50's—
rocks in swing. Keyboard
becomes a grand. Alto man
sweetens solo notes like reeds
waving on beach shore.

Bari burps and bellows basement
notes, a foundation of tone coupled
with the bass bone to settle a body
of sound into a nest of comfort.

Rhythm pumps beat with bass sock
and snare driving a highway chart
into sunsets of warm vibrations,
all bringing back distant dreams
of youth filled days—mostly nights.

Trumpets skirt the heavens
with high note fingering and
educated lips waking Gabriel,
who grabs his horn to dip
into the river of mystical emotions
that points up, soon for some.

The vocalist, half the average age
of band members, sings
I Get a Kick Out of You,
while the trombones blow
kisses back at her throaty
figure and body of vocalism.

Sassy sax's windy tunes send
melodies to our ears bringing
harmonious enjoyment.
This octogenarian band flies
with Michel Legrand scores
across the lake of life.

Dough for the Poor

I think I have to face the big issues, the life-and-death issues . . .
Thomas Merton

It matters not that life's rollercoaster causes gain or pain.
It's true, when you are in the pizza business all your life.
Dough from each pie rises to the mouths of hungry lame.

Son Victor starts as a worker of dough. He doesn't complain
and progresses to ownership of many stores by midlife.
It matters not that life's rollercoaster causes gain or pain.

He thrives with pies, weds a redhead, a son is his gain.
They find cancer in Sandy's womb and Vic loses his wife.
Dough from each pie rises to the mouths of hungry lame.

He works to aid the poor, those treated with wrongful disdain.
He raises his son and weds again, gains twins, bolstering life.
It matters not that life's rollercoaster causes gain or pain.

Wealth pores into their lives; they give more for humane
reasons, increasing their ethical standards to reduce strife.
Dough from each pie rises to the mouths of hungry lame.

It's clear that both forms of dough do enrich and sustain
their lives, but most-of-all open the door to a good afterlife.
It matters not that life's rollercoaster causes gain or pain.
Dough from each pie rises to the mouths of hungry lame.

Walleye Snapper

They used to call Catholics Mackerel Snappers—
you know, all that fish eating on Fridays. Mackerels
populate the North Atlantic and Walleyes live
in the Great Lakes, the Cadillac of lake fish.
And when eaten, your taste buds jump for joy.

If you introduce the joy of fishing to a young son,
chances are that you can eat fresh fish in your
older age at zero cost. Some sons become avid
bass fishermen—my oldest did. Today we feast
on a three pound Walleye because Phil is in town.

He visits each year in the spring, brings his sleek
bass boat to explore for schools of hungry fish
mostly in Lake St, Clair, the playground water
where affectionate fish are driven by glands
and tails to hunt for shore-line egg-producing mates.

Phil's fun lasts from 5 AM to 5 PM for four days
totaling 263 catches of which 233 are returned
to the lake to be caught by others in the future.
We wait for Phil to arrive home, as does the chocolate
cake that my wife has baked. Three walleye are gutted

and filleted after he gets home. Later we eat.
Phil says a prayer that touches my heart. It ends
with: *It is good to be in my father's house.*
Then we eat a delicious gift of walleye fish.
Phil leaves for Tennessee early the next day.

The metaphoric poetry of that prayer ending leads me
to write—the universe is expanding like God's love is.
Much good is done since people are healed, babies are
cared for, sons say good things and senior seniors
are guided from earth's transition to the Inventor of life.

An Eternal Thank You

Thank you God for the cosmos,
and including earth in it
and living things, some still
unknown to us, some yet
to become, some who are done.

Thank you for our minds. We humans
at times use it with your wisdom,
at times on issues without wisdom,
only our self-centered prosaic goals,
thus missing the point of our existence.

Thank you for being for all: your magnolia
trees, your fields of grain, your air we breathe
(not as clean as before), your sources of energy
to keep our babies warm, our toast tasty, our
computers flowing with helpful data—sometimes.

Thank you for making your presence present,
thereby letting us feel You in mind and heart,
coupled with You for a piece of time, for
peace of mind and heart. Yes, I repeat,
but You know I know your Love.

God's Love is Free

It is both divine lovemaking and human ecstasy.
Richard Rohr

God is free for me,
you too, if you just see
how this is true for thee.
Learn to open your heart,
to be smart.

God seeds our minds with need
for his love, to obtain the feed
that enables freedom to weed
fear, doubt and ego's mask—
a hard task.

With God, we can capture
freedom in Spirit—for grandeur
in soul and mind, spawning allure,
producing an ecstasy.
It's easy.

Fresh Bread in the Love Kitchen

He has a good heart; he's smart; he's considerate.
He loves his family, near and far, a love that
flows onto whomever he befriends in life.
Our son Michael wins with love, not combat.

Mikey, Mike's son, loves his dad because
Michael has poured his love onto his buddy,
becomes his mentor, his model, his giver
of guidance and teacher of humor and glee.

Mike worries about Lions and Tigers, Red Wings
and Pistons, Wolverines and Spartans. It seems
their offence, defense and records interrupt his dreams.
He does win contests by picking non-Detroit teams.

Mike owns a pizza store, runs it professionally
using high school kids, like a mom watching her kids.
They learn about ovens, dough, cheese, toppings
and how to please people without having sale skids.

During the aftermath of Katrina, he traveled
south to serve devastated Gulf people with bread
of pizza, baked in a mobile Love Kitchen van.
Hundreds of smiles were payment by those fed.

Mike loves his parents. His sensitivity for all brings
the spirit of the Spirit by handling stress with caress,
like a priest handles the bread and wine for his flock.
Mike's an artist that moves toward a life of calmness.

We Children of God

We children of God have it good.
We work to exhaustion to help our children.
Work of light begets clear sight,
letting each child think with open mind.

We work to exhaustion to help our children.
A daughter follows my path which aids her; she
lets each child see with open mind.
She flourishes under God's light and sun.

A daughter follows my path which aids her; she,
guiding the poor among us, with prayers for them.
She flourishes under God's light and sun.
The love felt is pure and without stain.

Guiding the poor among us, with prayers for them,
I also include my son's funds that aid their lives.
The love felt is pure and without stain.
They give their wealth for the survival of others.

I also include my son's funds that aid their lives,
that shows concern for all people and heals them.
They give their wealth for the survival of others.
Their families are first nearly all the time

that shows concern for all people and heals them
through deeds of love and dollars of service.
Their families are first nearly all the time
including when their businesses are challenged.

Through deeds of love and dollars of service,
I'm delighted about the quality of family fruit,
including when their businesses are challenged.
All six offspring are different with veins of truth.

I'm delighted about the quality of family fruit.
Work of light begets clear sight.
All six offspring are different with veins of truth.
We children of God have it good.

About the Author

Edward Van Slambrouck has written poetry at a prolific pace during his literary-ripe retirement years. Six children and eleven grandchildren put loving constraints on his time. As an engineer, he worked in the aerospace industry, which included computer programming for the moon rocket, Saturn. Later, he was brought on staff at Oakland University (Michigan) as a computer specialist, creating library systems and research tools and teaching some courses in computer science. He was also employed by General Motors Corporation. He completed his engineering career by establishing a computer training company, KETEC Inc. Nevertheless, Mr. Van Slambrouck continued to pursue the love-task of writing poetry throughout his adult life. He is member of The Academy of American Poets and The Poetry Society of Michigan.

In addition to writing poetry, Mr. Van Slambrouck plays his alto saxophone "to keep tuned to the music of life." During his youthful adulthood, he played saxophone in big bands and in combos. He sang in church choirs, both modern and classical scores, including Gregorian chant. Also, he is a lover of classical music and an avid aficionado of the original American music form—jazz.

OnSpring: A Family of Poems, Mr. Van Slambrouck's first book, a chapbook, was published in 2005. Peter Meinke, a noted national poet, commented the following about his chapbook: ". . . OnSpring, whose pages are heartfelt, moving, linguistically admirable and playful."

Mr. Van Slambrouck's second book, *Heart Music*, was published in 2008. Margo LaGattuta, a nationally known poet wrote: "With his musician's ear, Van Slambrouck brings us echoes of those diaphanous feelings that exist even in the silences between the words. Poetry is the perfect form for his thoughts because it combines sound and image in a way that is as close to song as one can get, while still using language."

His third book, *Opus in Chromatic Words*, was published in 2010. James Ahearn, the President of The Poetry Society of Michigan wrote the following: "Ed pays homage to his Creator and the Spirit of Love that is found between God the Father and God the Son. He transposes this relationship to his own life through religious faith expressed in various ways in many of his poems. What better method than this to fill that requirement."

Mr. Van Slambrouck lives in Orion, Michigan with his wife, Diane. He can be reached at vanslam30@yahoo.com. He asks readers to view his web site where he has displayed a set of poems: www.poetrywordmusic. wordpress.com

About the Editor

Carolyn Walker is a memoirist, poet, essayist, journalist, and teacher. Her creative nonfiction has appeared in The Southern Review, Crazyhorse, Columbia: A Journal of Literature and Art, The Writer's Chronicle, and Hunger Mountain, and her poetry in Encore, the anthology of the National Federation of State Poetry Societies.

Her essay "Christian Becomes a Blur" was nominated for a Pushcart Prize. Prior to obtaining her Master of Fine Arts degree in Writing from Vermont College of Fine Arts, Walker was an award-wining journalist, her work having appeared in numerous Michigan newspapers and magazines, including The Detroit News, The Flint Journal, and HOUR Detroit Magazine. She has received writing awards from the following organizations: Springfed Arts, National Federation of State Poetry Societies, Detroit Working Writers, Michigan Press Association, Suburban Newspapers of America, and the Association for Retarded Citizens.

Walker is the author of the creative nonfiction collection *A Mother Runs Through It*. She is a contributing author to the anthologies *Gravity Pulls You In: Perspectives On Parenting Children On The Autism Spectrum* and *At The Edge Of Mirror Lake*.

In addition to writing, Walker is a teacher of writing. She teaches for Writer's Digest University, AllWriters Workplace & Workshop, Springfed Arts, and Union Institute & University.

Walker is the married mother of three and she resides in Clarkston, Michigan.